LAND OF THE FREE

The Supreme Court

Anne Hempstead

Heinemann Library
Chicago, Illinois

Published by Heinemann Library
A division of Reed Elsevier Inc.
Chicago, IL
Customer Service 888-363-4266
Visit our website at www.heinemannraintree.com

For more information address the publisher:
Raintree, 100 N. LaSalle, Suite 1200, Chicago IL 60602

Printed in China by WKT Company Limited

10 09 08 07 06
10 9 8 7 6 5 4 3 2 1

ISBN 1-4034-7001-4 (hc) -- ISBN 1-4034-7008-1 (pb)

Library of Congress Cataloging-in-Publication Data:
Hempstead, Anne.
The Supreme Court / Anne Hempstead.-- 1st ed.
p. cm. -- (Land of the free)
Includes bibliographical references and index.
ISBN 1-4034-7001-4 (hc) -- ISBN 1-4034-7008-1 (pb)
1. United States. Supreme Court--Juvenile literature. I. Title. II. Series.
KF8742.Z9H315 2006
347.73'26--dc22
2005018873

Photo research by Julie Laffin

Acknowledgments
The author and publisher are grateful to the following for permission to reproduce copyright material:
p. 4 © Getty Images/Taxi/Peter Gridley, pp. 7 (a, c), 13, © Getty Images/PhotoDisc, pp. 7(b), 22 (tr) © Corbis, p.8 © Corbis/Reuters/Pool/Paul Sakuma, p.10 © Getty Images, p. 15 © Corbis/Royalty-Free, p. 16 © Corbis/Franklin McMahon, pp. 19, 22 (br) © Corbis/Reuters, pp. 20, 22 (bl), 25, 27 © Corbis/Bettmann, p.22 (tl) © Corbis/Stapleton Collection.

Cover: © Corbis/Zefa/Murat Taner

Every effort has been made to contact the copyright holders of any material reproduced in this book. Any omissions will be rectified in subsequent printings if notice is given to the publishers.

The paper used to print this book comes from sustainable resources.

Contents

Chapter One: Justice for All **5**

Chapter Two: The Beginning of the Supreme Court **11**

Chapter Three: The Court at Work Today **17**

Chapter Four: Making History **23**

Timeline 28

Further Information 29

Glossary 30

Index 32

Chapter One: Justice for All

"Oyez! Oyez! Oyez!" With this dramatic cry, nine justices in long black robes walk into the Court **Chamber** and the Supreme Court is brought to order. The Supreme Court is the most powerful court in the United States. It has the responsibility to make sure our laws follow the **Constitution**.

The Supreme Court is the name for both a building and a group of people. The building that houses the Court's chambers and offices is in Washington, D.C. The people are the men and women who serve as judges on the court. They are called the Justices of the Supreme Court.

The Supreme Court reviews and **interprets** the nation's laws. By making sure that the nation's laws follow the Constitution, the Supreme Court protects our rights as citizens and seeks to provide justice for all.

Interpreting the Constitution

The Supreme Court does not make the nation's laws. It only **interprets** them. Supreme Court justices can be compared to baseball umpires. Umpires do not make the rules, but when players argue over a play, umpires decide what the rules mean. Umpires interpret the rules to be sure the game is fair.

The **Constitution** established the rules of our government. When there are disagreements over the Constitution, the justices of the Supreme Court interpret the Constitution's rules. They decide if laws are **unconstitutional**, or not in line with the rules laid out by the Constitution.

Parts of the federal government

The writers of the Constitution divided the government's power into three parts or branches: legislative, executive, and judicial. The legislative branch, called Congress, makes the nation's laws. The president is part of the executive branch and enforces the laws by making sure that they are carried out. The judicial branch is made up of the Supreme Court and lower federal courts. The Supreme Court is the highest and most powerful court. It focuses on cases related to the meaning of the Constitution. The Supreme Court also hears a few cases that involve foreign **diplomats** and cases that involve events that took place at sea.

A System of Checks and Balances

Having three branches of government provides for a system of checks and balances. This means that no one branch will have too much power over the other two.

President's power

- *Enforces laws*
- ***Vetoes**, or overrules, bills from Congress*
- *Writes budget for the running of the government*
- *Appoints judges*
- *Makes agreements with other countries—with the approval of Congress*

Congress's power

- *Makes laws*
- *Votes on taxes*
- *Approves judges appointed by the president*
- *Has the power to remove the president or justices from office for misconduct*

Supreme Court's power

- *Makes sure the laws passed by Congress are constitutional*
- *Decides if actions taken by the president follow the Constitution*

The Supreme Court and the lower courts

The Supreme Court is located in Washington, D.C., the nation's capital. There are also lower **federal** courts located in each state. States also have a system of state courts.

Disagreements about the law and trials for breaking the law usually start in lower courts. If somebody gets a ruling, or decision, in a court that the person thinks is unfair, he or she can **appeal** the ruling. This means that the person takes the decision to a higher court to see if that court agrees with the first one. Depending on the situation, a person can appeal a case through lower federal and state courts, all the way up to the Supreme Court.

A lawyer argues a case before the 9th Circuit Court of Appeals in San Francisco. The 9th Circuit Court is a Federal Court.

Many cases that reach the Supreme Court make history. In 1942 the West Virginia Board of Education ordered that all its public school students must salute the flag. The board wanted to encourage **patriotism** and respect for the country. But saluting a flag is against Jehovah's Witnesses' religious beliefs. A group of children who were Jehovah's Witnesses refused to do it. The children were thrown out of school for not obeying the rules. Their parents took the case to the federal district court. The court ruled in favor of the parents.

The Board of Education appealed the decision. The Supreme Court agreed to hear the case because it raised questions about the constitutional principles of freedom of speech and religion. On Flag Day, June 14, 1943, the Court announced its decision. Six of the nine justices voted that state and local governments could not require anyone to salute the flag or say the pledge of allegiance. To do so was **unconstitutional**, because it violated the rights of free speech and religion.

Listen up

Oyez (pronounced "o yes") is said three times when a judge walks into a courtroom. It is based on a word in Old French meaning "hear ye" or "listen up." It has been used in English-speaking courtrooms for hundreds of years.

Chapter Two: The Beginning of the Supreme Court

On February 2,1790, the Supreme Court held its first session in New York City, which was the capital of the United States at that time. They first met in a former butchers' market. President George Washington appointed the first justices who were to serve on the court for life. However, in the early years of the court, the government had a hard time keeping justices on the job. Many turned down the position or quit after a short time.

One reason no wanted to be on the Supreme Court was that the justices also had to serve on the **federal** courts in their local districts. This meant months of travel back and forth on rough roads going from courthouse to courthouse. Another reason was that people were unsure about the job itself. The **Constitution** called for a third branch of government—the judicial branch. But there had never been a Supreme Court before. No one was sure what a Supreme Court justice did. If the president appointed the justices and the Senate approved their appointments, would the justices ever be able to make rulings that went against the people who had given them their jobs?

In 1803 the case *Marbury v. Madison* claimed that a specific act of Congress was **unconstitutional**. The Supreme Court, under the leadership of Chief Justice John Marshall, agreed. From that time on, everyone recognized the Supreme Court's right to decide if a law passed by Congress follows the **Constitution**. The Supreme Court had established its power.

The Court on the move

In 1791 the Supreme Court moved with the government to Philadelphia, Pennsylvania. Here the Court met in an unheated room in Independence Hall. When the government again relocated to the new capital city of Washington D.C., the court still did not have a permanent home. It spent ten years meeting in different places on Capitol Hill—from an unfinished room in the Capitol building to private homes and even taverns.

It was not until February 10, 1810, that the Supreme Court met in a **chamber** built for its use. The chamber, or room, in the Capitol building became the site of many famous debates. When Daniel Webster argued a case, congressmen flocked to the Chamber of Justice to hear him speak. It was reported that men even offered bribes to get the best seats in the Supreme Court chamber.

The Supreme Court was forced to leave its courtroom in 1812. War had broken out between the United States and England. When the British captured Washington, D.C., they set fire to most of the public buildings. The Capitol Building was burned to the ground. For several years, the Court again had to meet in taverns, homes, and even tents.

In 1860 the Supreme Court moved to the Senate chamber shortly after the Senate moved into a larger room. The old Senate chamber was better for the Court, whose sessions had become even more popular with the public. Two traditions from the early days of the court are still practiced today. One is that twenty white quill pens are placed on the lawyers' tables each day the Court is in session. Another is the judicial handshake. When the justices meet in conference or go on the **bench**, each justice shakes the hands of the other eight justices. This practice reminds the justices that despite their differences, all are members of the Court and share a common purpose: defending the Constitution.

Independence Hall, Philadelphia. One of the early meeting places of the Supreme Court.

The Court gets its home

The Supreme Court was 146 years old before it finally got its own building, in 1935. The Supreme Court Building is located on Capitol Hill across from the U. S. Capitol.

The building is designed to look like an ancient Roman temple. Its classical style matches the Capitol and other important government buildings. When Washington D.C. was first being planned, George Washington, Thomas Jefferson, and other leaders wanted the **federal** buildings to show that our government was based on the democratic ideals of ancient Greece and Rome. Cass Gilbert, the architect of the Supreme Court Building, followed the classical tradition. His design for the building gave the Court a dignified home that reflects the importance of the Court's work.

The building is made almost entirely of marble. The building is 92 feet (28 meters) high and takes up an entire city block. At the base of the 36 steps leading to the entrance are two statues of large, seated figures. One is of a woman and is called Contemplation of Justice. She represents what the justices do: think about the law. On the other side is a statue of a man. He represents the authority of the law.

At the top of the steps is a double row of sixteen columns supporting a porch. Above the entrance porch is a sculpture of eight men and one woman dressed in ancient robes and armor. The middle figures represent liberty, authority, and order. Some of the other figures were modeled after early justices and the architect, Cass Gilbert. The words "Equal Justice Under Law" carved above the entrance remind visitors that the Supreme Court's purpose is make sure that all American citizens have the same rights. The Supreme Court shows no favors or **bias** toward either side of a case.

Ancient Roman ruins, such as these ruins of a temple in Sicily, influenced the design of the Supreme Court building.

Chapter Three: The Court at Work Today

Huge bronze double doors, each weighing over 6 tons, open into the main corridor of the building, the Great Hall. The hall is lined with statues of all the former Chief Justices. At the end of the hall, oak doors lead into the Court **Chamber**. This is where the Supreme Court hears 80 to 100 cases a year. Each and every case is a test of the **Constitution**.

At one end of the Court Chamber is a long, raised desk called the **bench**. The justices sit behind this bench on nine black chairs. The Chief Justice sits in the center of the bench. To the left of the justices sits the Clerk, who manages the Court's **docket** and calendar for arguments. To the right, the Marshal of the Court keeps time and signals the lawyers with red and white lights telling them when their time is up.

Appearing before the Supreme Court is a great honor for lawyers. Before coming to court, lawyers for both sides have filed **briefs**, or summaries of their arguments. In court each lawyer has exactly 30 minutes to explain his side of the case to the **bench**. Usually much of the time is taken by the justices, who ask the lawyers one question after another. Later, after arguments have been presented and questions have been answered, the justices think about the issues, discuss the case as a group, and come to a decision.

Time's up!

In the early days, there were no rules for submitting briefs—in fact they weren't even required. In 1821 the Court established that each party coming to court needed to write down the facts of his or her case and outline an argument of why he or she should win. Lawyers took writing briefs seriously. Some produced summaries of their cases that ran 1,000 pages or longer. In 1980 the Court ruled that 50 pages was the limit. In other words—the court said to keep briefs brief.

In the beginning, there were also no time limits for **oral arguments**. Some could go on for days. In the late 1800s, the justices were known to go behind a curtain in back of the bench for lunch. They sat down and enjoyed their meal together while the lawyers continued arguing their case on the other side of the curtain.

A lawyer holds a press conference outside of the Supreme Court. Photos are not allowed inside the Supreme Court.

The court's work year is called a term. The term begins on the first Monday in October and continues until late June or early July. The term is divided into two-week "sittings" and two-week "recesses." When the justices are sitting, they hear cases and deliver opinions. The justices use recesses to think about the arguments they heard in cases and write formal opinions about cases.

Amendments

A decision by the Supreme Court can only be changed by another Supreme Court decision or by making an **amendment**, or change, to the **Constitution**. Before the 1950s, many Southern states would not allow African Americans and white people to attend the same public schools. In 1896 The Supreme Court upheld these laws. But the Court, like the nation as a whole, changed its mind. In 1954 it stated that **racial segregation** was **unconstitutional**. This ruling also overturned, or reversed, the Court's previous decisions.

When the Constitution does not cover a law that the nation wants, Congress can vote to add an amendment to the Constitution. In 1885 the Supreme Court would not let Congress put a tax of two cents per dollar on workers' earnings. This ruling was changed by the Sixteenth Amendment, which allowed Congress to call for an income tax.

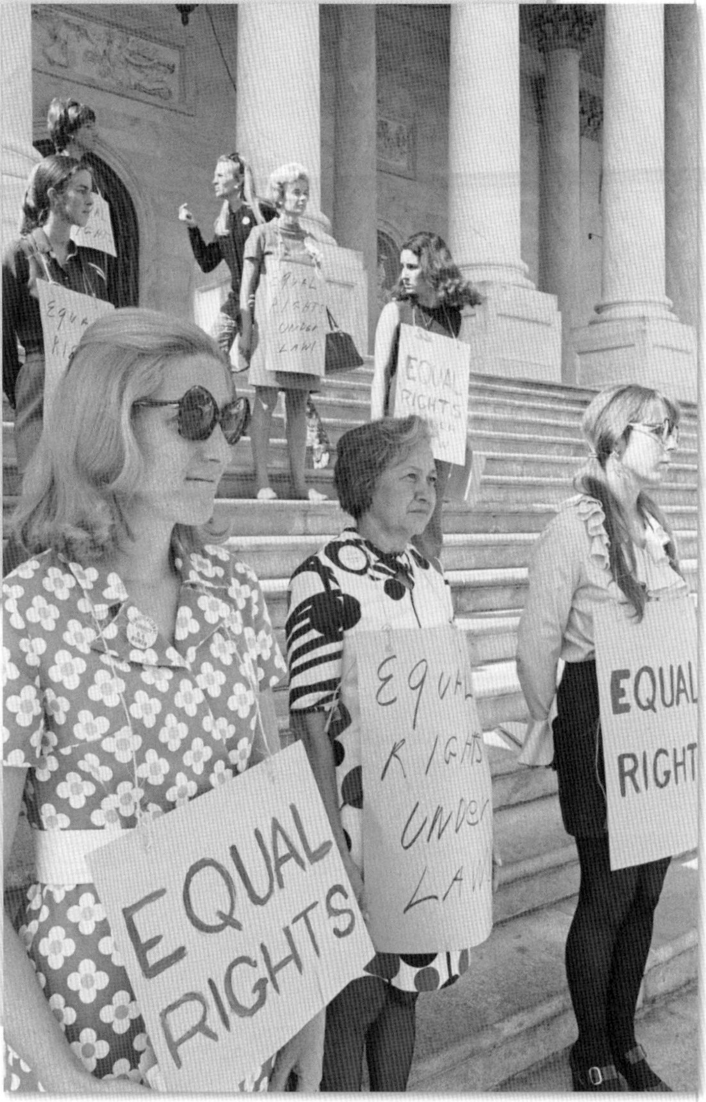

These women are protesting in favor of adding an Equal Rights amendment to the Constitution.

Making a decision

After hearing a case, the justices hold a private meeting to discuss it. These meetings usually occur on Fridays. The meetings begin with a handshake. The Chief Justice starts the discussion by asking each justice to give his or her opinion. A vote is taken with each justice having one vote. The justices do not all have to agree, but the majority wins. This means that with nine justices, the opinion held by five or more becomes the Court's ruling in the case—known as the majority opinion.

One of the justices clearly and carefully writes out the majority opinion of the Court. If a justice disagrees with the majority, he or she can write an individual opinion explaining why. These are called dissenting opinions. But the majority opinion is the final and last decision on the case.

The decision is read aloud in the Court. It is also published in a Supreme Court record called *The United States Reports*. Because the Court's decisions affect many peoples' lives, the decision are also often reported in newspapers, on the radio, and on television. Judges in lower courts use Supreme Court decisions to help them decide how to rule on similar cases.

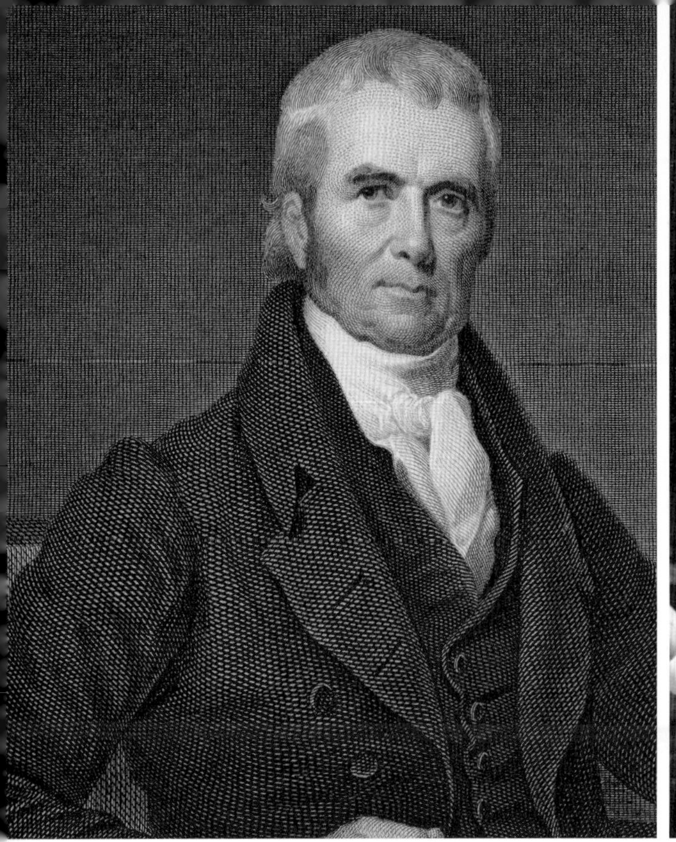

John Marshall

Oliver Wendell Holmes

Louis D.Brandeis

Sandra Day O'Connor

Chapter Four: Making History

The Supreme Court has nine justices who are appointed to life terms. When a justice resigns, retires, or dies, the U.S. president nominates a person to fill the opening. If the Senate approves the president's choice, the new justice is sworn in to serve on the court.

There are no special qualifications for becoming a justice of the Supreme Court. You do not even have to be a judge or lawyer. However, all justices have had law training and most have come from legal or political backgrounds. Some have been members of Congress, governors, or presidential cabinet members. One was even a former president, William Howard Taft.

John Marshall has been called the "Great Chief Justice." When he accepted the job in 1801, the Supreme Court's role in the **federal** government was unclear. Before his death in 1835, Marshall firmly established the role of the Supreme Court as the interpreter of the **Constitution**. He also strengthened the Court in other ways. In the early years, when the Court handed down a ruling, each justice delivered his own opinion. Marshall thought it was better if the Court acted as a unified, single-minded body. Marshall's writings were so clear and logical that many legal questions and Supreme Court decisions today still build on or refer to his decisions.

Justice Oliver Wendell Holmes Jr. disagreed with other justices so often he was known as the "Great Dissenter." Holmes strongly favored people's rights. He believed that the Constitution is a "living document" that needs to be interpreted according to the current time period. He felt that laws needed to change as people's needs changed.

Famous firsts

Louis D. Brandeis was the first Jewish person appointed to the Supreme Court. He came to the Court first as a lawyer arguing cases for clients. Brandeis introduced a new type of argument. Instead of arguments based entirely on what the law stated, he introduced facts and figures to explain what was really happening.

Thurgood Marshall became the first African-American Supreme Court Justice. As a lawyer he had won one of the Court's most famous civil rights cases—*Brown v. Board of Education of Topeka*. On the Court, he worked hard to protect civil rights and encouraged high standards of fairness.

Future training

Thurgood Marshall first became interested in the Constitution when he was a young boy. Marshall's principal sent students who misbehaved to the basement with a copy of the U. S. Constitution. They were instructed to learn a passage before they came back to class. In later life, Marshall said that before he graduated from that school, he had spent so much time in the basement he had memorized most of the Constitution by heart.

When Thurgood Marshall was a lawyer for the NAACP he argued cases before the Supreme Court.

In 1981 Sandra Day O'Connor became the first woman justice in the Court's 191-year history. Before becoming a Supreme Court justice, she worked as a lawyer and served as a state senator in Arizona. Justice Ruth Ginsburg became the second woman in history to be on the Supreme Court. O'Connor resigned from the court in 2005.

Landmark cases

The Supreme Court's rulings shape our country's laws. All of its decisions are important, but some are better known or more influential than others.

Dred Scott v. Sanford

In 1857 the Supreme Court ruled that Dred Scott, a slave, was not a U.S. citizen and had no rights in the United States. This decision deprived an entire group of people born in the United States of the rights due them as citizens. This case helped to bring about the Civil War. In 1868 the nation passed the Fourteenth **Amendment**. The amendment stated that if a person was born in the United States, or had become a citizen, he or she had equal rights with other citizens.

Brown v. Board of Education of Topeka

In 1951 an African American named Oliver Brown sued the school board in Topeka, Kansas. He wanted his daughter to be able to attend an all-white school near their home instead of traveling further to go to a school for African Americans. The Supreme Court ruled that segregated schools were **unconstitutional**. This ruling helped bring about other civil rights changes.

Miranda v. Arizona

In 1963 Ernesto Miranda was arrested in Arizona. The police questioned him for two hours. They did not tell him he had a right to remain silent or to have a lawyer present. At trial Miranda was found guilty. In 1966 the Supreme Court overturned the lower court's ruling. The Court said that the **Constitution** guarantees that everyone is entitled to a lawyer. It also said suspects must be read their rights before being questioned by the police. These rights are now known as "Miranda rights."

Ernesto Miranda and his lawyer. Miranda's Supreme Court case made history.

Texas v. Johnson

In 1984, during the Republican Party's national convention, a man named Gregory Lee Johnson protested the president's policies by burning an American flag. A Texas court found Johnson guilty of breaking state law. In 1989 the Supreme Court ruled that the First Amendment protects a person's right to burn the American flag. It also said the Constitution protects the right to express a personal or political idea even if other people find that view offensive.

For more than 200 years, the Supreme Court has had an impact on the way we live. The Court has worked to keep our nation's laws fair. As the guardian of the Constitution, the Supreme Court is one of our most important symbols of freedom and democracy.

Timeline

1787 The United States Constitution is written creating the Supreme Court

1790 Supreme Court meets for the first time

1800 The Court moves to Washington, D.C.

1857 In *Dred Scott v. Sanford*, the Court declares that slaves are not U.S. citizens.

1868 Fourteenth **Amendment**, making the Supreme Court's *Dred Scott* decision **unconstitutional**

1896 In *Plessy v. Ferguson*, the Court decides that the policy of "separate but equal" facilities is constitutional.

1935 The Supreme Court moves into its new building in Washington, D.C.

1954 The Supreme Court, declares that the "separate but equal" policy in schools is unfair and unconstitutional.

1967 Thurgood Marshall becomes the first African-American justice

1981 Sandra Day O'Connor becomes first woman on Supreme Court.

2005 Chief Justice William Renquhist diesand John Roberts is appointed Chief Justice.

2006 Justice Sandra Day O'Connor retires. Justice Samuel A. Alito, Jr is confirmed.

Further Information

When a Supreme Court justice retires the President of the United States nominates his or her successor. The president usually nominates an experienced judge whose writings and opinions agree with the president's views. The justice's appointment is voted on by the Senate Judiciary Committee. A majority of senators has to vote to accept the nominee in order for the nominee to become a justice.

For more information on how the Supreme Court works, and how you can visit the Supreme Court go to www.supremecourt.us.gov

Further Reading

Britton, Tamara L. *The United States Supreme Court.* Edina, MINN: Abdo, 2004.

DeJohn, Heather. *The Chief Justice of the Supreme Court.* Farmington Hills, MINN: Gale Group, 2002.

Glossary

amendment change to the Constitution

appeal request for a new hearing of a case

bench office or position of a judge. Also the seat a judge occupies.

bias unfairly favoring one side in an argument

brief summary of the facts and arguments to be used by a lawyer in preparing a court case

chamber government meeting room or official's office

Constitution rules and principles that establish the U.S. government

diplomat government official who works with people from other countries to solve problems and strengthen international relationships

docket list of court cases to be heard

federal government that divides power between a central overall government and the individual powers of the states

interpret to explain the meaning of words or ideas

oral argument explanation a lawyer presents in court to explain why a case should be decided in favor of his or her client.

patriotism love for and pride in your country

racial segregation policy of separating people by race

unconstitutional not following the rules and principles of the Constitution

veto overrule a proposed law, bill, or amendment to the Constitution

Index

amendments 20, 26, 27
appeals 8
architects 14

bench 17, 18
Brandeis, Louis D. 24
briefs 18
Brown, Oliver 26
Brown v. Board of Education of Topeka 26

Capitol building 12
Capitol Hill 12, 14
chambers 12, 13
checks and balances 7
Chief Justices 12, 17, 21,24
Clerks 17
Congress 6, 12, 20
Constitution 5, 6, 11, 13, 17, 20, 24, 25, 27
Court Chamber 5, 17

decisions 18, 20, 21.
designs 14
dimensions 14
diplomats 6
dissenting opinions 21
docket 17
Dred Scott v. Sanford 26

federal courts 8, 11
First Amendment 27
Fourteenth Amendment 26

Gilbert, Cass 14
Ginsburg, Ruth Bader25
Great Hall 17

Holmes, Oliver Wendell, Jr. 24

income tax 20
Independence Hall 12
interpretation 5, 6

Jefferson, Thomas 14
Johnson, Gregory Lee 27
judicial branch of government 6, 7, 11
judicial handshake 13, 21
Justices of the Supreme Court 5, 6, 9, 11, 12, 13, 17, 18, 21, 23, 24, 25

lawyers 13, 17, 18, 24, 25, 26

Marbury v. Madison 12
Marshals of the Court 17
Marshall, John 12, 24
Marshall, Thurgood 24, 25
Miranda v. Arizona 26
O'Connor, Sandra Day 25
opinions 19, 21, 24
oral arguments 18

presidents 23

quill pens 13

Scott, Dred 26
Senate 11, 13, 23
Sixteenth Amendment 20
state courts 8
Supreme Court Building 14

Taft, William Howard 23
Texas v. Johnson 27
time limits 17, 18

The United States Reports 21

Washington D.C. 5, 8, 12, 14
Washington, George 11, 14
Webster, Daniel 12
West Virginia Board of Education 9